Seven Principles of Good Government

Gary Johnson
on Liberty, People and Politics

SILVER LAKE PUBLISHING

ABERDEEN, WA • LOS ANGELES, CA

Seven Principles of Good Government
Gary Johnson on Liberty, People and Politics

First edition, 2012
Copyright © 2012 Gary Johnson

Silver Lake Publishing
P.O. Box 173
Aberdeen, WA 98520

For a list of other publications or for more information from Silver Lake Publishing, please call **1.360.532.5758**. Find our Web site at **www.silverlakepub.com**.

Library of Congress catalogue number: Pending

Gary Johnson
Seven Principles of Good Government
Gary Johnson on Liberty, People and Politics
Pages: 152
ISBN: 978-1-56343-913-1

Table of Contents

Seven Principles of Good Government

From the beginning of my two terms as governor, I faced a lot of skepticism about my "unconventional" approach to public policy. Not that I cared so much.

Introduction

My name is Gary Johnson. In 2012, I'm running for the office of President of the United States.

I base my decisions, both personally and professionally, on seven principles that I've derived from my experiences as the son of a school teacher, the owner of a large construction company, a two-term governor, a competitive athlete, and a husband and father.

I learned early on that there's no "they" lurking out there to keep us down…or come to our rescue. It's you and I who are going to get the important things done.

My seven principles have worked and continue to work in every aspect of my life. To stay focused and true to these principles, I keep them written down on a small piece of paper in my wallet. They are:

1. Become **reality-driven**. Don't kid yourself or others. Find out what's what and base your decisions and actions on that.

2. Always be honest and **tell the truth**. It is extremely difficult to do any real damage to people who are willing to tell the truth regardless of the consequences.

3. Always **do what's right and fair**. Remember, the more you accomplish, the louder your critics become. Learn to ignore them. Maintain your integrity and continue to do what's right.

4. Determine your goal. **Develop a plan to reach that goal. Then act**—don't procrastinate.

5. Make sure **everyone who ought to know** what you're doing, **knows** what you're doing.

6. Don't hesitate to deliver bad news. **Acknowledge mistakes immediately.** There may still be time to salvage things or to make corrections. Take Henry Kissinger's advice: "Anything that will

be revealed *eventually* should be revealed *immediately*."

7. Be willing to do whatever it takes to get the job done. If your job doesn't excite you enough to follow this principle, resign and **find a job you love enough to do what it takes**.

The seven principles outlined in this book explain how I conduct my life, my business and my campaign to restore liberty and prosperity to America. They explain how I will approach the vital task of bringing government and its spending under control, and reinstituting individual freedom and opportunity as the foundations of this great nation.

But, as important as these principles are, decisions about public policy and how to spend tax dollars must be based on something even more fundamental. They must be based on a clear vision of the proper role of government. Before deciding how a program should work or how much we should spend, the first question must always be: Should government even be doing it in the first place?

As simple as it sounds, Democrats and Republicans alike long ago stopped asking that question. We hear much about cutting government spending, balancing the budget, and the old standard: cutting waste, fraud and abuse. But, if you listen closely, these promises are almost never made in the context of making government actually *do less*.

Instead, when you wade through the rhetoric, you are hearing the politicians promise to keep government doing the same things—just cheaper. That approach, as we have seen via decades of Administrations and Congresses, doesn't work.

Rather than just debating how much government should or should not be spending and taxing, we need to be taking a hard look at what government is doing. I would strongly suggest that, if we roll back what government does and restore it to a proper role—a constitutional role, spending and taxes will largely take care of themselves. It is a great deal easier to spend less when we have less to pay for, rather than foolishly trying to spend less without reducing what government does.

And when we reduce government to its proper and limited role, freedom and opportunity will grow.

My view of the proper role of government is straightforward:

Government should protect you and
me from those who would do us harm,
threaten our rights, and take away our
civil liberties, whether they be foreign
or domestic enemies, unscrupulous
businesses and corporations, or
individuals.

It is *not* the proper role of government
to manage our daily lives, decide what is
best for our families, impose values on our
communities and institutions, or determine
winners and losers in the marketplace. While it
is the duty of government to protect us from
external threats and sometimes one another,
it is not the role of government to protect us
from ourselves.

And it is certainly not the proper role of
government to intervene in the affairs of
other sovereign nations simply because we
don't approve of them or somehow believe we
should shape them in our own image.

I frequently say, often to raised eyebrows,
that good government is easy. It is, if we
maintain a clear view of government's proper
role and apply a few straightforward principles
by which to fulfill that role.

Seven Principles of Good Government

My parents, Earl and Lorraine Johnson, my sister Lori, my brother
Scott and me (standing, right of center)—around Christmas, 1968.
We were a no-nonsense family. My parents lived in the Dakotas
early in their marriage but settled in Albuquerque, New Mexico,
when I was a young boy.

in Idaho and then running through the gates and checking my times.

My first run was 16 seconds and my next was 15.25. I tried it again and got the run down to 14.5. Still not fast enough.

On the lift back up the mountain, I rode with a ski patroller who pulled out a joint, and we got high before we got back to the top of the course. I felt like I really aced the next run and had gone faster than before.

But my time was actually 18 seconds, much *slower* than I had skied before the joint.

It was an epiphany for me. Getting high wasn't what I thought it was. It really impaired my judgment. And it wasn't going to get me where I wanted to go.

I stopped smoking on a regular basis.

Starting Out in the Real World

I graduated from UNM in 1975 with a bachelor's degree in political science, married my college sweetheart Denise "Dee" Simms, and started my own business, which eventually became Big J Enterprises.

I'd always been a good skier and wanted to take a shot at making it as a professional. A lot of ski pro's in the west work construction in the summer, since that can be a reliable way to make good money quickly. So, I followed that model for a few years.

Eventually, though, it became clear to me that the money I was making in construction had more long-term potential than my split times on the slopes.

Near the end of college, I'd been working construction for a contractor who built from the ground up. It was good fortune for me: I learned electrical, foundations, masonry, sheetrock, framing and painting.

But the contractor ran out of work, and I needed about 30 dollars a week to get by. So, I started looking around for other jobs.

One day, when I came home, there was a flyer on our doorstep from a kid who wanted to rake our leaves. It was a simple and effective way to advertise—and a *kid* had done it. I thought, "I'll do this for construction."

And that's what I did. I passed out circulars door-to-door that read, "College student needs work. Will do carpentry, painting, cement, anything and everything." That was the origin of Big J.

Working for the contractor, I'd been making about $3.50 an hour, which was pretty good money for a college kid. So all I had in mind was matching that $3.50 an hour.

I had garnered up my fifth job, which was to spread rocks out all over this man's yard. I remember thinking it was going to take about 22 hours, so I told him I'd do it for $80. He agreed. I showed up on Saturday morning thinking I would work all day Saturday and all day Sunday. I started at 7:30 a.m. and, by 10:30 a.m., I had finished the job.

I was nervous. I thought there was no way the guy would pay me what turned out to be more than $20 per hour. I didn't know what to do. And I couldn't think of any other way to be busy because the rocks were already spread.

So the man walked out, and my heart raced. He told me I'd done a great job and handed me a check for $80. I remember looking at him, looking at the check and thinking, "This is the American way."

At that point I knew I would never be employed by anyone again. I wanted to run my own business.

Earning Independence

I'd majored in political science at the University of New Mexico, partly so I could find out how to run for office. I learned that, practically speaking, money and ideas were the two most important ingredients in politics.

I had a lot of ideas, and I wanted to share them and work to help them become reality. I could see that, to achieve a position where I could enact my ideas, I needed my own money—so as not to be beholden to other people and special interests.

I viewed public service as a high calling, one in which I could do good by people.

At several points when I was still just getting started in business, I thought about running for state senator or city councilman. But I decided that a long record of voting and positions on various issues would have its pluses and minuses. I wanted to go in with a clean slate and fresh ideas on the issues that confronted our state and country.

I also wanted to wait until I had the resources to finance my own campaign.

So I wondered: how much money did I have to make?

I decided to break it down into real, tangible numbers. To make a million dollars in a year, I figured, I would have to make $3,500 to $4,000 per day, or $400 to $500 per hour. If I had a lot of people working for me, and they were all making a profit, it could be done.

But I knew it would be hard work.

I started by focusing on improvements and expansions to people's houses—and marketing with those same, simple fliers. In time, we expanded into commercial building projects. With a lot of help from many dedicated employees, we grew Big J Enterprises into a multi-million-dollar corporation.

By the time I sold the company in 1999, it was one of New Mexico's leading construction companies, grossing between $20 million and $30 million per year. We had grown from a door-to-door business to a multi-million dollar corporation, ranked as high as number 34 on the New Mexico Private 100 companies list.

When I sold the business, I made enough money that I wouldn't have to work ever again.

I'd earned true freedom.

Seven Principles of Good Government

An early campaign picture. I didn't know enough not to run for governor...and win.

Chapter 2: My Time in Public Office

In the early 1990s, I decided it was time to dive into public service. I introduced myself to the Republican Party two weeks before I entered the governor's race. When I approached the Republican Party about running for a top statewide office, party officials politely dismissed me, telling me an unknown businessman could never win.

In fact, at early political gatherings I was often snubbed and openly laughed at for what I was doing. When my profile ran in the *Albuquerque Journal*, the summary listed my birthplace and birthday, my residence, education and occupation. And then, under political/government experience, it said "None."

The *Journal* article went on to state:

> In one sense, his lack of experience might be his greatest campaign asset. In another, it makes him a political gamble.

But my ideas resonated with voters who were as frustrated as I was with crime, taxes, a growing government and the "can't do" attitude of state leaders.

Here's how one of my rivals in the primary remembered that election in an interview with the online magazine Slate.com:

> "I sized him up as a total neophyte and somebody who had no chance," remembers John Dendahl, who got into the Republican primary later and had much more government experience than Johnson. "But he spent a lot of money. He bought a lot of ads on the sides of buses in Albuquerque, and he acquitted himself very well in the debates. ...At one of the debates, the candidates got asked how we'd deal with the Democrats in the legislature. New Mexico is

basically two-to-one Democratic, you
see. Johnson got that question and
said he'd veto them. Now, most of us
laughed at that. We didn't have enough
Republicans to sustain the vetoes!"

But we won enough seats in the legislature
to sustain the vetoes. And I used that pen
against legislative schemes. A lot.

I ran for governor as the owner of a
successful construction company with no
political experience whatsoever. When the
Republican ballots were tallied in 1994, I'd won
with 34 percent of the vote in a four-way race.

Of the $540,000 I spent in the primary,
$510,000 of it was mine. I did not solicit
donations because I did not want to be
beholden to anyone or any group. It was easier
to focus on my message instead of having to
be worried about fundraising.

I said this many times, and I still believe that
people who would have given me money would
have expected certain things from me. They
would have wanted, or even demanded, my
signature on legislation that I ultimately vetoed.

I had individuals who'd supported me
financially upset with my vetoes of their bills.
On a few occasions, I offered to refund their

Seven Principles of Good Government

contributions, but I was never taken up on my offer.

Right or wrong, I could not have gotten involved in politics at an earlier stage because I didn't want to feel indebted to anyone. I wanted to be in an independent position.

Focusing on Issues, Not Opponents

I ran my first campaign, as well as my reelection campaign, in a unique way—never mentioning my opponent in print, radio or TV. It was awesome. I did not even allude to the fact that I had an opponent. I stayed 100 percent on message; and it worked.

My message was a simple: individual freedom, individual rights and less government run with a common-sense business approach.

I opposed public funding of abortion and federal land management control, and I supported lower taxes, term limits, tough criminal sentences, gun ownership rights, right-to-work legislation and public funds for school vouchers.

I wanted to make certain that liberties and freedoms are equally available to all, with a limited government which basically ensures that no one is harmful to anyone else.

My overriding philosophy was, and still is, a common-sense, business approach to state government and putting important issues on the front burner regardless of political consequences.

Best product, best service, lowest price.

Shocking the Conventional Wisdom

As an outsider and against all odds, I defeated incumbent Democratic Governor Bruce King by a ten-point margin at a time when registered Democrats outnumbered registered Republicans two-to-one in New Mexico.

To win my second term, I had to beat the strongest Democrat in New Mexico, the popular Mayor of Albuquerque, Martin Chavez. I debated him 28 times. I didn't have to, but I believed that's what the people deserved—to hear the issues.

I believe I beat Chavez all 28 times.

I told the people that I would not get along with the legislature and that, if they wanted someone who got along with the legislature, they shouldn't vote for me.

I didn't and don't seek endorsements because they are not important to me.

Seven Principles of Good Government

In the 1998 election, I increased my share of the vote by five percent, making me the first governor in New Mexico history to be elected to two consecutive four-year terms.

During my two-term tenure as governor, New Mexico experienced the longest period without a tax increase in the state's entire history.

Some of my other accomplishments included:

- reducing taxes $123 million annually;
- cutting the historic rate of state government growth in half;
- leaving the state with a budget surplus and 1,000 fewer employees (without firing anyone);
- privatizing half of the state's prisons;
- shifting state Medicaid to managed care, cutting the historic growth rate in half and creating a better health care network in the state;
- defeating campaign finance legislation;
- increasing the percentage of the state's budget devoted to improving the state's education system eight straight years;
- overseeing the construction of 500 miles of new highway.

Gary Johnson on Liberty, People and Politics

I became known for my libertarian, common-sense approach to governing. And I earned the nicknames Gary "Veto" Johnson and "Governor No" (I prefer "Governor *Know*") by vetoing 750 bills. I may have vetoed more bills than all of the other 49 governors in the country at the time. Combined.

Those 750 vetoes didn't include line-item vetoes in state budgets, which I raised to an art form. It was safe to say that I had the most contentious relationship with my legislature of any governor in the country.

These are some of the facts of my time as governor. But, sometimes, people ask me to describe the governing philosophy that compelled me to take so many hard lines on public policy issues.

I didn't mind for a moment saying "No" so often. I believe that every time you pass a law you take a little bite out of freedom.

Although I do not believe that government is ill-intentioned, I strongly believe in less government. The government has not been effective in anything it decides to do, and government regulations have precipitated much of the trouble we face today. I vetoed 750 bills as governor because I abhor the government spending our money on programs that show no improvement in our lives and criminalize actions that do not warrant criminalization.

In cases where the government must oversee services, I favor privatization and competition.

I vetoed "hate crime legislation" that literally scares me to death because it prosecutes thoughts, not actions.

During my tenure, we reduced taxes by about $123 million annually. More significantly, before my taking office there had never been eight consecutive years in the state of New Mexico where not a single tax went up.

The Philosophical Frame

I agree with the CATO Institute—a non-partisan organization that promotes public policy based on individual liberty, limited government, free markets and peaceful international relations—on most issues, including immigration, free trade, marriage equality and opposition to the Iraq war.

CATO grades governors, giving them a report card every two years. Some governors ranked first one year and then fifteenth the next. Although I was never the top-ranked governor, I consistently ranked among the nation's top seven in each of CATO's fiscal report cards between 1996 and 2002.

And I was proud (as well as a little surprised) to be the only politician to be invited to speak at CATO's annual conference in October 2009.

To me, good government is getting better goods and services at the same or better price.

Staying competitive requires seeking quality goods and services at the lowest possible price. Basically, the government's role should be to protect us and our property from physical harm. It's a humble mission—but more difficult than most people realize.

Unfortunately, the government's role has grown too large.

Seven Principles of Good Government

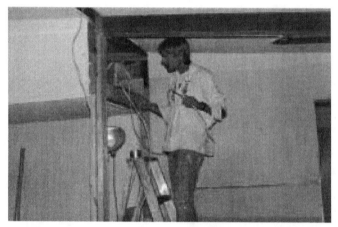

An early picture of me, working as a handyman. A couple of good breaks near the end of college put me on a path toward a solid knowledge of the construction trade. And toward starting my own company, which I built into one of the largest contracting firms in New Mexico.

Chapter 3:
What I Believe

My overriding philosophy is the common-sense business approach to government, period. Best product, best service, lowest price.

Without exception, I am a civil libertarian. I believe in the supremacy of individual rights and personal freedoms above unwarranted government interference or control.

Overall, I think I view big government in the same way that the novelist and philosopher Ayn Rand did—that it really oppresses those that create, if you will, and tries to take away from those that produce and give to the non-producers.

Seven Principles of Good Government

But I believe in a strong national defense.

The attacks on September 11, 2001, were horrific. And we should be at war with al Qaeda—the transnational terrorist group which seeks to destabilize and destroy the United States.

I don't believe our national security is being threatened in either Iraq or Afghanistan. I believe the torturing of individuals has created tens of millions of enemies for our country that we might not otherwise have had.

I voted for President George W. Bush twice, but I was the only Republican governor not to endorse his bid for the presidency during his first primary.

I endorsed Steve Forbes, instead. I liked his ideas about a "flat" federal income tax.

I don't think George W. Bush ever had to stand in line in his life. That gave him a perspective most people don't have. And certain limitations as a leader.

He didn't understand the plight of common people.

Bush's terms as governor of Texas overlapped with mine in New Mexico. I think he was the governor who attended the fewest meetings of the National Association of

Governors—and I think I was the governor who attended the most.

I have always said that 80 percent of the meetings were a waste of time, but you could never predict when the lights would come on and a good idea would present itself.

My Issue: Drug Legalization

In 1999, I became the highest-ranking elected official in the United States to advocate the legalization of marijuana. I realize this is not a politically popular view.

Ignoring the drug issue would be more politically expedient. In fact, advocating such a thing as legalization of marijuana could be political suicide. But I cannot sit back and remain silent when I see a way to reduce death and disease, crime and corruption, and do the right thing for our country.

The responses I got in the governor's office—calls, letters, faxes, emails, people talking to me on the street—to my position on marijuana were about 95 percent positive.

The reaction from elected officials, on the other hand, at least officially, was 100 percent negative. But I have been approached by some elected officials who've said, "Way to go. This needed to be said. Your position is right, but I can't say that in public."

I'm willing to risk my political future to educate people and bridge the divide.

I believe that most—maybe 90 percent—of America's drug problem is related to prohibition, not use. I don't mean to discount the problems of use and abuse, but I do believe we Americans should redirect our government's focus.

Like most things, the best drug policy comes down to cost-benefit analysis: What are we spending and what are we getting for it?

My assessment is that the war on drugs is a miserable failure. I don't know of a bigger problem in every single state, or a bigger expense that might actually have alternative solutions.

Drug prohibition accounts for over half of law enforcement spending, half of prison spending, and nearly half of court spending.

What are we getting for it? Almost two million arrests annually and overcrowded courtrooms and prisons.

I recently met with a group of judges at a conference in Oregon, and they overwhelmingly agreed with my position.

Petty drug offenses cost too much and crowd the legal system. The judges told me that methamphetamine is the best example of what law enforcement experts call a "prohibition drug."

In other words, the judges said, if cocaine were legal (and they were not advocating that it should be), most drug users would never resort to meth. It probably wouldn't even exist.

But it does. And, because meth is cheap and relatively easy to make, it harms the poor disproportionately.

I believe we should start with legalizing marijuana, and then look at harm reduction strategies for other drugs. We need to look at the issue first and foremost as a health issue, not a criminal justice issue.

I'd like to think my drug stance had something to do with the fact that, while I was governor, legislative trends across the country stopped escalating the penalties on drug crimes. Legislation stopped getting tougher. It didn't get better—but at least it didn't get worse.

That seems to be a good start because drug abusers need treatment, not incarceration.

My message to my own kids has always been: I love you both, first and foremost. If you find yourself impaired in any way, call me any time to come and pick you up, no questions asked.

Seeing It Through Their Eyes

When I was governor, picking up trash was a passion of mine. I regularly went out and picked up trash with troubled teens. Once I was out on trash duty with 24 teenagers who were all in treatment for marijuana, and I started talking to them. These kids shared with me their love of smoking pot. One kid said he wanted to get married, have kids, sit on the porch and smoke pot. "But I have to stop now, or I'll go to jail," he said:

> I'm doing my community work, taking the mandatory tests and all that, but as soon as I'm done here, I'm going to smoke pot again. We all are. I'm just going to be more careful this time.

The kids, at least the ones who would openly discuss it, substantiated my position.

We spend all this time, money and effort on trying to get kids and others to stop smoking pot, and they're not going to!

I think it's harder for kids to get alcohol right now than it is to get pot.

I will never advocate kids doing drugs or legalizing kids' drug use. But I believe there would be less of a supply on the street—and kids would have a harder time getting the stuff—if marijuana were legal.

When my stance on drug legalization came out, I was the butt of late night jokes and my favorability in New Mexico plummeted from 58 to 28 percent. But, in the name of drug enforcement, doors (often, the *wrong* doors) are getting kicked down every day in the United States and our civil liberties are being trammeled.

I'm as good at making the argument for legalization of marijuana as anyone I know. And I will continue to be an advocate for the issue because it's the right thing to do.

I'm proud that my favorability returned to 58 percent before I left office four years later, having advocated the legalization of marijuana.

Reflecting on Two Terms in Office

I'm also proud of what we were able to accomplish during my time as governor. Regardless of political consequences, I put important, even controversial, issues on the front burner and confronted them head first.

Seven Principles of Good Government

I had a "Mr. Smith Goes to Washington" experience because I did what I should have done without worrying about political penalties.

When my tenure as governor was over, I was known for my common-sense business approach to government. And I could not have written a better description than that.

A Few Last Observations

When I'm out on the campaign trail, people sometimes ask me about my religious beliefs. My answer's simple: I was raised a Lutheran. I think I have Christian values. I don't attend church.

I support marriage equality. But government shouldn't be involved in marriage in the first place.

As governor, I put people before politics, confronted the tough issues and did what I thought were the right things. If you asked people on the streets of Albuquerque about me today, they may say they disagree with what I did. But I think they would all agree that I am principled and honest.

And, perhaps most important, I believe that anybody who's willing to be an entrepreneur in this country can make an absolute fortune.

Gary Johnson on Liberty, People and Politics

Backstage with my campaign strategist, Ron Nielson, and television talk show host Sean Hannity. While Hannity doesn't pretend to be a libertarian, I've always found him to be a decent guy. Which is a rare thing in his line of work.

Giving a quick interview to southern California radio station KROQ at an event supporting marijuana legalization.

Seven Principles of Good Government

On the slopes with my daughter, Seah, in the early 1980s. Though I never turned pro, skiing has remained one of my life's passions. And that passion influences how I operate even off the slopes.

Chapter 4:
How I Operate

My whole life has been driven by goals and the little steps required to reach those goals. For me, life is a journey, not a destination. And in the Land of Enchantment, which is New Mexico, many of my dreams have come true.

Perhaps my most wide-ranging media interview during my time as governor was one that I did with *Reason* magazine in early 2001. It carried the headline "America's Most Dangerous Politician."

When the magazine asked me to describe my approach to governing; I said:

> I'm a cost-benefit analysis person:
> What are we spending and what are
> we getting? . . . the war in drugs is a
> miserable failure. . . .We are arresting 1.6
> million people a year in this country on
> drug-related charges, and it's a failure.

When *Reason* asked me what I thought
my biggest achievements in office were, I
answered:

> Building 500 miles of four-lane highway
> in the state.
>
> We have reduced taxes by about $123
> million annually.
>
> More significantly, before my taking
> office there was never a set of eight
> years in the state of New Mexico where
> not a single tax had gone up.
>
> We reformed Medicaid and got Medicaid
> costs under control.
>
> We built a couple of new, private prisons
> in New Mexico. We had prisoners
> housed out of state, and the federal
> court system had been running prisons
> in New Mexico under a consent decree
> since 1980. We are now out from under
> that consent decree.
>
> We have approximately 1,200 fewer

employees in state government today
than we did when I took office.

After My Two Terms Ended

Since leaving office, I have spent much of
my time skiing, biking, competing in several
triathlons and being an outspoken advocate of
physical fitness.

Athletics have always been a main joy in my
life.

Fitness has gotten me through several
rough points in my life. One, especially, comes
to mind.

Big J's big break came in the mid-1980s,
when we got the contract for an Intel Corp.
plant expansion. That deal boosted revenues
from a couple million to over $30 million.

Sounds great, right? It was good. But it also
created all kinds of stress and difficulty.

I spent my days making collection calls just
to meet the company's growing payroll and
expenses. And the pressure of that, every day
over the course of many months, took a heavy
toll on me. Emotionally and spiritually. I got to
the point that I felt like I understood suicide.

I took a time management course in 1987.
There, I realized—looking back over my life—

that when I was fit everything seemed to work. So I stopped drinking and decided to be in the best shape of my life every day of my life.

I decided that I wanted no handicaps in my life. I wanted and needed to be all I could be.

I made it a goal to climb the highest mountain on each of the seven continents. I've done four and have three—Vincent, Carsten Pyramid and Acancagua—still to go.

Competition and Fitness

When I was first elected governor, I attended the National Governors Conference and went running with Ed Shaefer, the governor of North Dakota. Soon after, Shaefer let it be known that he was relinquishing his title as the fittest governor to me.

I'm proud of how physically fit I am.

After my time as governor, I hiked and skied every day.

In January 2003, we got a lot of new snow and I skied right into a stump that was buried underneath. Somehow I got down the mountain and went to Mogul Medical in Taos. At first the doctor told me that I couldn't have broken my leg because if I had I never would have made it down the hill.

An examination proved otherwise. My tibia was fully fractured, and my injured leg was six to eight inches bigger than my other leg. I was devastated because I had plans to climb Mount Everest in the spring.

Jim Liebowitz, an orthopedist for the U.S. Ski Team, told me I could make it to Everest if I used an experimental bone-healing device, took no pain-killers or anti-inflammatory drugs and started therapy in the swimming pool the next day.

It worked.

Eight weeks later, I left for Nepal with a healing leg. I had two more months before reaching the summit, so I knew it would continue to heal.

The climb was a memorable project. My daughter was able to spend some time with me as we prepared at the base camp.

My friend and expedition leader Dave Hahn and I made it to the 29,035-foot summit on May 30, 2003; and, despite some mishaps (including frostbite due to poor circulation in my healing leg), the experience was unbelievable.

It was absolutely exhilarating to stand at the top of Everest.

A New Passion

In 2004, I stayed at Point of the Mountain in Utah for several weeks, and took up paragliding in a really big way. The next year, I went to Hawaii to test my skills.

On the morning of October 13, 2005, I took off first from a tight spot and immediately flew into some trees that I had been flying over for weeks. I broke my back, damaged my knees, tore my ACL and broke three ribs.

I ended up walking out of the Hawaiian hospital and got on a plane two days later bound for New Mexico for treatment. When I got off the plane and to the neurosurgeon, he thought I was crazy. I needed surgery and two and a half years to fully recover. I haven't been paragliding since, but I plan on doing it again.

My Greatest Project: My Children

In 2005, my children—Seah and Erik—and I went to climb Russia's Mt. Elbrus, which at 18,481 feet is the highest peak in Europe. We spent some time in Europe before the climb and then joined nine other climbers and two guides to scale Elbrus.

My daughter Seah is in her early 30s, lives in Albuquerque and works in technical theater.

When she left home to attend the University of Colorado at Boulder, I gave her $1,500 to spend for the semester. I had already paid for her room and board, so I told her that she could see how long the money lasted and we would talk about what she needed as she ran out. The days and weeks went by, and Seah never mentioned money.

When she came home for Christmas, I asked her why she never called for more money. She told me she still had $1,300 left!

I had given Seah our old Ford Explorer to take to school. One day she was driving to Arizona and, on the way, the car broke down near Gallup, New Mexico.

She said she knew it was the alternator, so she hitchhiked into Gallup, got the parts she needed, and fixed the car herself.

I told her that she didn't need to be so frugal, that college should be fun, that she should go out and have a good time once in a while. She told me, "Dad, I'm having a great time! There is nothing I'm not doing that I would like to do. I'm fine."

She graduated as valedictorian.

Seven Principles of Good Government

My son Erik is in his late 20s. One of the best things that happened to me while I was governor was getting to watch how Erik developed during that time.

At home in Albuquerque, he had not been doing well in school and was placed in several remedial classes. But, when we moved to the state capitol, Santa Fe, he excelled and made honor roll.

I don't think the classes were any easier, I think he was just able to rise to the occasion and figure out what he needed to do.

Another instructive story about Erik: He went all the way through high school with very few of his schoolmates ever knowing that he was the governor's son. It was important to him to fit in as normally as possible.

And he did.

Erik has become a wonderfully engaging young man. He graduated from the University of Denver and works for a company called eCollege, where he makes college courses accessible online.

Gary Johnson on Liberty, People and Politics

Since I left the governor's office, I've built upon my association with the CATO Institute, which I consider one of the most effective libertarian think tanks in the U.S.

Announcing my bid for the Libertarian Party nomination and throughout the campaign, I've used the slogan "LIVE FREE." It usually doesn't need much elaboration.

Seven Principles of Good Government

I've completed several Ironman Triathlons. These intense races test your mind as much as your body . . . and teach you a lot about overcoming adversity.

Chapter 5: Adversity

The years 2005 and 2006 were a tough period for my family.

My wife, Dee, and I had met when we were teenagers skiing at Red River (a popular resort near the New Mexico/Colorado state line).

We got along great, right away. When we got married in 1977, after we'd both graduated from UNM, I was very happy to have Dee as my wife, as my great friend, and as the woman I'd spend my entire life with. And we had many great years together.

But, as I look back on it now, I can see there were some cracks in the foundation of the relationship—even early on. In order to get along with Dee, I believed that I couldn't always tell her how I really saw things.

I avoided telling her things because the stress was too much for her, and her reaction to it was too much for me.

So, I started telling her white lies to smooth things over. Not big lies or lies about important things, just little lies. Lies of omission. About the progress of a house we were building, for instance, or a decision I'd made at work.

Later, when I got into politics, the little white lies were about the issues I had to deal with as governor. And then the effects of the stress and the lies started to show. I'd been living with lies for a long time; it had become the only way I knew to get through the day.

When I realized that telling the truth had taken a backseat to convenience, I quit lying—which created terrible situations of blame and anger. But I just couldn't live any longer as I had been. Not speaking my mind completely, leaving things out.

When it comes to relationships, I've always liked the saying "If one side of the mirror is always angry, the other side becomes angry, too." Our marriage had become a mirror with two angry sides.

I realized I wasn't really living up to the principles I had outlined to myself years earlier as my core beliefs.

I wasn't being honest to all people at all times because I wasn't being honest with my wife. I needed to tell the truth and have my partner be able to hear it.

It took me a long time to come to terms with all the little lies that I'd told Dee and, when I finally did, we'd grown too far apart. Our marriage had dissolved.

Difficult Choices...and Circumstances

I initiated a separation in May 2005, after 28 years of marriage; we divorced soon after.

Then, a little more than a year later—on December 22, 2006—Dee died tragically and far too young of hypertensive cardiovascular disease.

Here's how the *Albuquerque Journal* reported Dee's obituary:

> Former New Mexico first lady Dee Johnson has died, her family announced. Johnson died peacefully in her sleep at her Taos home. She was 54. "We are devastated by this sad news," the family statement read. "She was really look-

ing forward to spending Christmas with the family and close friends. We ask that everyone keep us in their prayers."
Former Gov. Gary Johnson said the death was "very sudden" and a total surprise to friends and family. "She was an outstanding human and cared about everyone she came across," Johnson said in a telephone interview about his ex-wife.

"People couldn't have gotten a better number one volunteer, because that's what she was," Johnson said of her time as first lady. "Whatever (the issue) was, she had a caring approach."

…Johnson avoided the public spotlight for most of her reign as first lady, saying in 1995 that she preferred solitude and anonymity to public appearances.
She graduated from UNM with a degree in elementary and special education.

I wish I had said or done something sooner to repair the foundation of our marriage.

If there was a casualty to my time as governor, it was my relationship with Dee. And I'm sorry for that. I loved Dee. I still love her parents and family.

To this day, I have terrible bouts of guilt about the divorce.

A silver lining in all the sadness of those years was that, when Dee passed away, she left our children her half of the money we'd made during our marriage.

From their mother, my kids inherited financial independence. Their freedom. And an important element of personal liberty.

Seven Principles of Good Government

Aloft in a balloon with Richard Abruzzo. Ballooning with this guy wasn't a wine-and-cheese affair; it was every bit as intense as a major mountain summit. Richard tragically died in 2010 when his balloon went down in the Adriatic Sea.

Preparing before the Fox News Presidential Debate, Fall 2011.

Gary Johnson on Liberty, People and Politics

My mom, Lorraine, and me, before my senior prom in 1971. In high school, I was a good athlete and an adequate student.

Next to skiing, one of my main passions in life has been bike racing. This picture, taken when I was governor, promoted our statewide program to clean up roadside litter.

Seven Principles of Good Government

After a couple of tough years in 2005 and 2006, I've been able to emerge in a pretty good place.

Chapter 6:
My Life Now

I believe in relationships.

Since the divorce and Dee's death, I've been involved with a couple of women. I dated a doctor for about three years; when that relationship ended, I made it a goal to find someone new as quickly as reality would allow. I put together a list of women I knew with whom I thought I might be able to build a relationship.

Near the top of that list was Kate Prusack, a real estate agent I'd met in competitive biking circles.

When I first met Kate, she was in a long-term relationship. But, a few years later, a mutual friend told me she'd broken up with her boyfriend. So I called her.

I was nervous. I left a long phone message, wondering whether she had any interest in a relationship with a 55-year-old ski bum.

She called me back, politely telling me that she *had* broken up with her boyfriend—but they'd gotten back together. She was bright and polite. And thanked me for the call.

I was sad to hear that. I went back to my list and the rest of my life.

Then, about three months later, Kate called me back. She'd broken up with her boyfriend again. For good, this time. And she would love to see if a relationship was possible.

We've been together pretty much ever since.

Kate is beautiful, she's athletic, she's smart. We're in love. I asked her to marry me while we were on a chair lift at Taos.

At one point, early in our time together, Kate asked me about my politics and political philosophy. What it was, how I'd come to it.

I gave her a copy of *Atlas Shrugged*.

Kate and I each wear a engagement ring. Those rings might look just like wedding rings to a casual observer (some reporters on the campaign trail have made that assumption).

And that's okay with me.

In the meantime, we bought a house in Santa Fe and we're excited about our future together.

A Memorable Trip

In 2008, Kate and I went to Africa and climbed Mount Kenya and Mount Kilimanjaro with Seah, her partner Josh Phillips and Erik.

Together, the five of us felt like a close-knit unit. Like a family.

That trip was important for me. It felt like my kids and I had emerged from a difficult period. We were all well and happy again, for the first time in a long time.

The trip allowed me to see more clearly than ever that time moves fast. Using time well is so important to living a full life. And getting important things done.

This is one of the reasons that I'm such a stickler about being on time.

Running a business was about being on time, keeping my word and doing more than expected. Being governor was about getting the right things done. Climbing Mount Everest was about being capable of doing it, not just getting to the top. Running for president is

Seven Principles of Good Government

about the ultimate challenge of being relevant and involved.

Through all of these experiences, I have developed my seven principles of good government, which guide my actions not just in politics—but personally and professionally as well.

A great thing about living in the southwestern United States is the combination of an outdoor lifestyle and serious interest in politics and policy. You can meet incredible people hiking or biking.

Gary Johnson on Liberty, People and Politics

Strategist Ron Nielson, Matt Welch, editor-in-chief at *Reason* magazine, me and David Nott, president of The Reason Foundation. I enjoy talking with people like Matt and David; but it can be unnerving for them. They're not used to talking with politicians who share so many of their policy views.

Another shot of me on a bike. This was another leg of our anti-littering tour. The promotion also let New Mexico kids see that even an "old" person like the governor can stay fit.

Seven Principles of Good Government

Talking to a student group. I visit campuses a lot; and I always stress the importance of being reality-based. This is a message college kids don't hear often enough.

Chapter 7:
Reality

Principle: Seek reality and base all your decisions and actions upon it.

Back in 1993, I was seriously considering running for the United States Senate.

Lew Campbell, a prominent attorney in Albuquerque, got wind of my desire and asked me to go to lunch. He wanted to know if it was just a publicity stunt, or if I was serious.

I assured him I was serious, and he asked me if I knew what a U.S. Senator really does. "No," I replied.

"Neither do I," he responded, "but I think you'd make a better governor."

Campbell convinced me that I couldn't get the Republican nomination for U.S. Senator. He convinced me to run for governor instead.

Seven Principles of Good Government

Even if I came across as flaky to my friends, I didn't want to run if I didn't have a real chance. I wanted to get into politics so I could make a difference, and to do that I had to *win*. Reality dictated I had a better chance at winning if I ran for governor. So I did.

Prisons

At the time, the single biggest issue in New Mexico was the prison system. The courts had ruled that New Mexico prisons were woefully incompetent to carry out their functions. A consent decree forced the federal government to oversee the state facilities.

Approximately 700 prisoners from New Mexico were being housed out of state due to prison wing closures resulting from federal oversight. This put prisons at the forefront of my agenda.

The New Mexico legislature did not want to address the prison issue. It had become an enormously expensive and embarrassing situation. Reality dictated that something had to be done to solve the problem in an economically and politically-palatable way. With this perspective, I figured that if we went to a privatized system, we wouldn't have to come up with the funds and it would cost only two-thirds of what it was costing the state.

Public control of the prisons cost about $76 per prisoner per day, and private control cost about $56 per prisoner per day. We were able to provide the same services and still run the prisons with those significant savings. The system is still running that way today

Education

Reality dictated that New Mexico public education needed a serious overhaul as well.

I promised to increase the percentage of money the state spent on K-12 education as well as on higher education. While I was governor, we increased the percentage of budget that we spent on K-12 every year.

But, beyond the money, by all measures students were doing a little bit worse from year to year. The budget had constantly increased, so it seemed to me that students should have been doing at least a little bit better.

Although we were spending more money, we weren't getting a better outcome. So, privatization seemed to be an attractive alternative here, too. I believed that vouchers would allow families choices they wouldn't otherwise have. I proposed that every K-12 student in the state of New Mexico, all 300,000 of them, get a $3,500 voucher to attend whatever school the family wanted.

I realized that many people believed vouchers take money away from the public school system. But my plan would have increased the per capita funding for kids who remained in public schools because we were actually spending about $5,500 per child—so each public school district would get an extra $2,000 for each student who opted out.

I used this example to explain: If every student in Santa Fe were to opt out of public schools, which would never happen, Santa Fe public schools would be left with about 40 percent of their budget and no students. Tell me how that takes away from public education.

The argument that vouchers favor the rich is also absurd. People with money live in good neighborhoods that have good schools. Vouchers are for the poor, for those that don't have money, who live in the worst neighborhoods, go to the worst schools, and can't get away from them.

The argument that vouchers are unconstitutional because you're giving money to private schools is also bogus. If you want to start calling vouchers unconstitutional, then every single state has got a lot of unconstitutional programs. We give low-income parents money so they can take their pre-school children to day-care centers of their choice. Many are church-affiliated. We don't tell them where they have to take their child.

I believe that we should treat K-12 education more like higher education. The reason higher education in the United States is the best in the world is because these institutions compete with each other for tuition dollars. We need that same competition in public education.

This is not about getting rid of or weakening public education, it's about providing alternatives that will force public schools to react very quickly. Public schools will get better if they have to compete.

Promoting New Ideas

Vouchers were unpopular in New Mexico, but that didn't stop me from telling the truth about the need for competition in our school system. And, although my voucher plan didn't pass, the debate resulted in more charter schools and more discussion about improvements besides increased funding.

When it comes to issues like prisons, education or road construction, I'm convinced you get the best product at the lowest cost when private enterprise injects competition into the process. That's just reality.

Another bill I vetoed was the dog and cat exercise bill that would have required pet store owners to exercise their dogs and cats at least two hours per day. At first glance, it sounds like a great idea. And, if a pet store regularly exercised its pets, that's where I would want to shop. But we don't need a law *requiring* pet exercise! Then we would need enforcers and penalties for those who didn't comply.

The Death Penalty

When I was younger, I supported capital punishment. I changed my mind because I recognized that the risks and costs associated with the death penalty are too high.

I understand the eye-for-an-eye, tooth-for-a-tooth mentality but, realistically, public policy should have room for mistakes. Killing one innocent person who was wrongly accused is not worth executing 99 guilty people.

DNA evidence and judicial appeals have shown that many people are mistakenly convicted.

In Illinois, after a number of death-row inmates were freed on appeal, Gov. George Ryan ordered a legal review of every prisoner on death row. That uncovered so many questionable convictions that Ryan ultimately commuted the death sentence of *every* prisoner on death row in that state.

In New Mexico, the Vagos motorcycle gang was convicted of brutally killing a gay man in Albuquerque, and two men and one woman were sentenced to death and spent over ten years on death row. Then, a different man confessed to a priest who came forward with information only the killer would know; and the Vagos members were released.

In Texas, the Vagos gang members would already have been put to death because of a time limit on death penalty appeals.

Cases like these made me realize the death penalty is flawed public policy and its consequences are irreversible. Plus, the financial cost of capital punishment (mostly legal fees) is several times greater for taxpayers than keeping someone in prison for life.

Not one innocent person should be put to death to punish those who are guilty. I found out the reality of the issue and based my stance on that.

Reality is also the basis for my advocacy of legalizing marijuana. America's war on drugs has miserably failed.

You would think that with its permissive marijuana laws, The Netherlands would be the cannabis capital of the world. In fact, that is not true. We have greater per capita drug use in the United States than they do in The Netherlands.

Reality Can Be Tough

Despite tougher drug policies in the United States, Americans are twice as likely to have tried marijuana than the Dutch. Researchers found that 42 percent of people surveyed in the United States had tried marijuana at least once.

There's some evidence suggests that attitudes are shifting:

- According to Gallup Poll released in October 2011, 50 percent of Americans support marijuana legalization. Only 46 percent oppose it.

- In Massachusetts, the people voted 65 to 35 to decriminalize the possession, sale and use of marijuana.
- In a Denver referendum, the citizens voted to decriminalize possession of marijuana. The basis of the campaign was that marijuana is safer than alcohol.

There have been other votes in Nevada (three years ago) and in Alaska (six years ago), with the same general numbers: about 57 percent against legalization, and about 43 percent in favor of legalization.

This is a real turning point in America.

Every year in the United States, we arrest about 1.8 million people (nearly the population of the entire state of New Mexico) for drug-related crimes. Half of these arrests are for the possession of drugs, and half of the money we spend is for law enforcement, court and prison for drug-related crimes.

The myth is that people using drugs are degenerates. The truth is that most marijuana smokers are people we associate with every day—law-abiding, tax-paying, productive citizens.

Bad personal decisions should not be criminal if they don't harm anyone else. It is and should always be illegal to drive while you're impaired or to commit crimes. But people will always use drugs. We can't change that.

Our real focus should be on reducing death, disease, crime and corruption.

These problems are all related to drug prohibition, not drug use.

But what I've found is that most people base their position on this issue on emotion instead of facts.

The truth is that marijuana is safer than alcohol. I'll be the first to tell you that the world would be a better place if no one drank or did drugs.

But that will never be the case.

Give People Freedom...and Choices

As far as I'm concerned, you can get blitzed every night of the week as long as you don't drive or adversely affect other people.

I think your life would be better if you didn't and, in fact, I haven't had a drink in 22 years. But you should be able to do what you want to do if you're not harming anyone else.

Although I don't advocate legalization of drugs other than marijuana, a Swiss program for heroin addicts illustrates the positive effects drug legalization can have.

In Zurich, the Swiss government runs a successful heroin maintenance plan for addicts who get a prescription for heroin from their doctors. They get their heroin at a clinic and actually ingest the heroin under a doctor's supervision. Clean needles mitigate AIDS and Hepatitis C, and controlled quantities and impurities diminish overdoses.

Since the prescribed heroin is so much cheaper than it is on the street, addicts don't engage in crime to get it and they lose their motivation to recruit other addicts to pay for their own habits.

Zurich's police chief had been the leading opponent of this heroin maintenance program but, after witnessing his city's crime rate sharply decline, he became the program's leading proponent. Heroin addicts get safe, legal doses and don't resort to prostitution or other crimes to pay for them. They can be productive, job-holding members of society.

This is a much better situation than the one we have in America today with tens of thousands of addicts obsessed with where and how they are going to get their next fix, and how they are going to pay for it. We all pay a heavy price for that every day.

One last issue that needs a dose of reality is our country's approach to Social Security and other entitlement programs. I've been on the record about this problem for years.

As ABC News noted in 2010:

> Citing a story in *USA Today* which reported that a rash of retirements in 2009 is pushing Social Security to the brink, Johnson…said the retirement age needs to be raised perhaps to 70 or 72. "This is the reality, we're broke," said Johnson. "We're broke."

That's *still* the reality.

Gary Johnson on Liberty, People and Politics

I've always enjoyed getting off the beaten track that establishment candidates tread.

Seven Principles of Good Government

This exchange at an Occupy Wall Street event started off a little tense. But the kids relaxed when they realized I was going to hear what they had to say without judging them. So much of retail politics is listening . . . and getting people to *believe* they've been heard.

Chapter 8: Honesty

Principle: Be honest to all people all the time.

Mahatma Gandhi said that enlightenment is when what you think and what you say matches up with what you do.

When I really think about my life and the reasons I've had success, it all comes down to the basic principle of telling the truth. Truth in business, truth in relationships, truth in public office, truth in everything.

I always remember a placard I saw when I was young that read, "If you tell the truth, you don't have to remember anything." I've tried to take that notion to heart, and I've found that there couldn't be a more truthful statement. Even as a kid, I tried to choose friends who told the truth and, when they stopped telling me the truth, they weren't my friends anymore.

I have had times in my life when the truth took a back seat, and it was not a good thing. The fact is that my divorce was, in part, caused my inability to tell the truth to my wife.

As difficult as losing her has been, I know that going forward honesty will be paramount. I will never allow myself to deviate at all from the truth.

I think, as a presidential candidate, that will be something really different.

Honesty and Growing Children

A few years back, my son Erik was attending the University of Denver. He called to tell his mother and me that he was going to a social event in Aspen and would be staying at a motel there with his girlfriend.

Dee was beside herself, insisting that it wasn't right or moral to be doing such a thing. I looked at her and expressed my opinion about the news: Although I wasn't excited about it, I was grateful for the fact that he was telling the truth.

I told Dee that we could preach about morality and have him resent us, or we could listen and be glad he was telling us the truth. I, personally, would rather have him feel comfortable telling the truth than creating an environment in which he would lie.

Honesty and Marijuana

When I was running for governor, a reporter asked me if I had ever smoked marijuana. I hadn't been asked that before, so I was caught a little off guard. But I answered that, yes, I had smoked marijuana. And inhaled. And that I had even tried cocaine on a couple of occasions. I told the truth.

My consultants were up in arms and wanted to meet with the editors to talk about it. As it turned out, I could not have written about it better myself.

The front-page profile piece in the *Albuquerque Journal* ran, describing my drug use in the context of who I am—that I'd tried it, and that I didn't apologize for that.

I'm still not apologizing for it because I think people would rather elect a person who has experienced life. I knew my opposition would jump on it, especially because the election was in 1994 and, although a lot of people had smoked pot, no one was admitting it in those days.

As expected, the opposition attacked. Not only did I smoke weed, they claimed, but I wasn't sorry and wasn't taking things seriously enough.

In fact, the Lieutenant Governor candidate at the time, Patricia Madrid, had done her share of pot smoking. She would not admit her drug use and preached about my bad example for kids. When her pot smoking eventually came out, she was caught like a deer in the headlights.

Her hypocrisy played in the media for weeks, and she got crushed.

President Barack Obama also smoked pot. He has called it a youthful mistake and during his 2008 campaign recanted his 2004 promise to legalize pot.

I believe pot smoking was a non-issue in my case because of my honesty about it. There is power in the truth. The worst sin, the sin that is so entertaining, is hypocrisy.

It was not New York Governor Eliot Spitzer's affinity for prostitutes that damaged him (as a politician, if not as a TV talker) but the fact he'd prosecuted so viciously prostitutes and those who used their services.

President Bill Clinton did not suffer much from his affair with Monica Lewinsky, in my opinion, because he was never a moralist. And, so, he wasn't a hypocrite.

Honesty and Business

In August 1994, during my first campaign for governor, a reporter for the *Albuquerque Journal* called to ask me whether I'd faked a pressurized pipe test on a Big J Enterprises construction project a short time earlier.

I said I had not, but the next day an enormous headline proclaimed "Big J Fakes Pipe Test." It was as big as the headline that had declared "Man Lands on the Moon." And it was accompanied by a detailed diagram showing how the test had been faked.

That morning I hopped in an airplane at 5:00 a.m. and got to Hobbs, New Mexico by 7:00 a.m.

I had more than 1,000 employees at that point and didn't know who specifically was responsible for the test. I started an investigation. It quickly became evident that the test had, indeed, been faked.

The next day, the site foreman didn't show up for work, which confirmed my suspicion that he'd been the critical person involved in the shady dealing.

So, I contacted the media and conceded that it appeared the article was correct—and the test had been forged.

Although I had no further knowledge of what had happened, I took full responsibility. The next day's headline read, "Johnson Says It's True," along with the details of my response.

The third day's story, "Johnson Orders Pipe Test," focused on the remedies we were pursuing, and the fact that the site foreman had quit. (I gave the media the ex-foreman's contact information, but he never responded to their questions.)

The whole episode cost me about $50,000, to re-test the pipe and deal with the media fallout. But I knew—and everyone else knew—that the pipe had been tested and was working properly. A week later, the headline announced, "Pipe Test Okay."

You'll never go wrong by telling the truth. Never.

As governor, I told my cabinet: If any of you get yourselves in a situation where we've made a mistake, I don't want us to ever make the statement that we can't comment because of legal restraint. We need to comment.

We need to tell the truth all the time. And we'll let the lawyers catch up with the truth.

Another example of honesty being the best policy is what I call the "tunnel scandal" while I was governor. My Corrections Secretary designee reported to me that there was a tunnel system under the state penitentiary site.

Instead of verifying that, she reported it to the media, and the story played in the news. It turned out that the so-called "tunnels" were, in fact, heating pipes that were part of the HVAC system.

We looked completely stupid; but we told the truth about our mistake and, after a day or two, the story had run its course.

Learning from Mistakes

Another mishap that we endured during my tenure as governor was misprocessing extraditions from other states. A woman in my office misprocessed about six extraditions, which would have meant that dangerous criminals would have been let free. The press descended on my office and wanted to know who was responsible for the potentially egregious error.

Although my advisors wanted me to point the finger and fire the employee who had actually done the paperwork, I took the blame and responsibility for not properly training her. The criminals were never actually released, so no harm had come from her errors. I then made sure she got a lot of training, so it would not happen again.

Two weeks later, she made the same mistake again, and I had to let her go. But, again, I saw from this experience that telling the truth and owning up to your mistakes always has a better outcome than trying to cover things up.

At National Association of Governors meetings, I was often asked to give advice to other governors. I told the old and new governors that one key to success is to always tell the truth to the press.

I remember saying that once, and I saw four or five governors lean back in their chairs and look at me like I was crazy. Their body language screamed, "What planet are you from?" Most agreed with me, but I think it is very easy for politicians to say and do things to stay in office.

The Advantages of Honesty

My experience taught me that telling the truth was actually a great way to stay in office, minimize criticism and garner respect. If you were to ask people in New Mexico today what they think of Gary Johnson, I think they would say that although they might not have agreed with some of my policies, they knew I was honest with them.

I'm very proud of the fact that I always told the truth, regardless of the consequences or unpopularity of what I was doing.

When I told people my stance on legalizing marijuana, some thought I was crazy, even if they agreed with it. "What's the point of creating a headache for yourself that you could avoid by keeping it to yourself?" they asked.

The answer: I believe truth is proactive. You shouldn't withhold truth until you're asked exactly the right question in exactly the right way.

The principle of being honest to all people all of the time applies to politics, business, personal relationships—all aspects of life.

During my years running Big J, we worked with thousands of people in Albuquerque.

Seven Principles of Good Government

You would think that, during my campaign for governor, a few nasty letters to the editor would surface complaining about the lousy job my company or I had done, or about someone feeling they were ripped off or cheated in some way. People *expect* that these things happen in every business.

Not one complaint surfaced because these things didn't happen in my business.

Although respected by many, my honesty has been an alienating force at times. I'm not asked for my opinion in New Mexico as much as I used to be, and candidates do not ask for my endorsement mainly because of my stance on legalizing marijuana.

I'm not sought out because I'm controversial—in the sense that candidates don't want to alienate any potential supporters. And I'm fine with that. What a luxury not to have to comment on every issue of the day!

When you tell the truth, no one can damage you. And the worst damage is minimized by telling the truth.

Gary Johnson on Liberty, People and Politics

An early campaign event in New Hampshire. As people in New Mexico know, and those across the country are learning, I am a truth-teller. Even if the truth is going to hurt some.

Seven Principles of Good Government

Another talk with students. It often impresses me how many young people are receptive to rational arguments for limited government. They know instinctively that the bureaucrats in D.C. are bankrupt, both morally *and* fiscally.

Chapter 9:
Focus

Principle: Acknowledge your critics, but do what's right.

I will not bow to my critics or compromise my beliefs—but I always go out of my way to explain the reasons behind my beliefs.

My theory is that often criticism results from poor communication and misunderstanding. If you explain your positions well, you can further your position and diminish criticism. You must be aware of your critics, but proceed with your beliefs.

Not acknowledging his critics was one of President George W. Bush's biggest problems. He ignored his critics based on what he thought was the truth; but he turned them off by not even communicating with them.

Again, the issue of legalizing marijuana is a huge lightning rod.

I have critics galore. Mostly because of this.

I think marijuana and alcohol handicap our minds. Our reactions are slowed, and our mental and physical capacities are impaired. But just because marijuana and alcohol are handicapping doesn't mean we should go to jail for using them.

We should end up in jail for drinking and driving impaired, drinking and committing a crime, or drinking and harming someone. We should also end up in jail for smoking marijuana and driving impaired, smoking marijuana and committing a crime, or smoking marijuana and harming someone.

Those are the lines we need to draw, and no more.

But if you examine the failure of the war on drugs and look at the alternatives as I have, you might come to the same conclusion.

I acknowledge my critics and take the challenge of going out to every nook and cranny in New Mexico and the United States to explain my views. When I left office, I had a 58 percent approval rating, even after advocating legalization of marijuana. I don't ignore or avoid criticism, it spurs me on to communicate better.

School Vouchers

The issue of school vouchers is similar. A poll came back that said we shouldn't use the term "voucher," that we should use "choice" or "opportunity scholarship" instead. But we were talking about vouchers!

I didn't want to try to circumvent or dilute the issue. Instead, we took it to every part of the state, to the teachers' convention, to the parents, and made our case that, with so much money pouring into our schools, we had little to show for it. Competition would make our schools better.

I endured constant criticism, but I confronted it head-on with facts.

When I sought re-election, my opponent thought the school voucher issue would be the death of me. It wasn't.

Without exception, I am a civil libertarian. I believe in the supremacy of individual rights and personal freedoms above unwarranted government interference or control. Critics of my approach abound, but I've stuck to many unpopular positions.

Despite critics' proclaiming my insensitivity, I vetoed a $250,000 program for high school drop-out intervention under the premise that we had a school funding formula in place and existing school officials, not another state-funded program, should deal with the drop-out problem.

Bringing a Business Mindset to Policy

My views are in the minority for many key policy issues, but I strongly believe in certain principles and hold to my beliefs.

Business is about "Best product, best service, lowest price." If you can combine all three of those elements, then you're successful. Period.

We're spending a lot of money on education, but I don't think it's an issue of money. As Americans, we spend more and more money on a product that, by all objective measurements (test scores, drop-out rates, etc.), is doing a little bit worse each year.

Is there any other aspect of our lives where we're allowing this gradual failure to happen? I don't think so.

The public education system in the United States needs major reform.

In order to improve schools, we have to measure and grade schools. And the purpose here isn't to denounce the schools but to say, "All right, here's where we're at. What do we need to do to get better next year?"

We need to compare one school to another when it comes to test scores in the various categories. We also need to be able to look at one school from one year to the next, and have the results put out in a format that is easy to read and easy to understand.

A solid education makes a big difference when it comes to jobs, when it comes to health, and when it comes to your own personal well-being.

You're not going to get ahead unless you're as well-educated as you possibly can be.

I see vouchers as a way of bringing those three business elements into education: Best product, best service, lowest price.

Vouchers Have Momentum

The momentum is clearly in the direction of people saying, "You know what? We've got to give vouchers a chance. There is something to this. This makes sense." It has become a campaign issue because people recognize it's a no-lose proposition: The voucher is redeemable at public schools, so what is there to lose? Other than some really bad schools that won't be in existence any longer.

Here's an observation: In a room of 1,000 people, ask "How many people here know of people over the last year who have gone from opposing vouchers to now believing that there might be something to vouchers or, in fact, support vouchers?"

You'll have a bunch of hands go up, perhaps as much as half the room.

Then ask the question, "Is there anybody here that knows of somebody who has been supportive of vouchers and that, over the course of the last year, is now *not* supporting the concept of vouchers?"

No one will raise his hand. I mean, *nobody* raises their hands.

I've got news for anybody who criticizes vouchers as being unconstitutional or says that government can't be spending money on religious institutions. In essence, we have a voucher system for child care. For those mothers who are on welfare, we give them what in essence is a voucher which allows them to choose where to send their children to child care, and in many cases that child care is religious. That's a state-funded program. We don't call it a "voucher" but we might as well.

Perhaps one of my most comprehensive interviews about my position on education reform was an on-the-record talk I had with the great George Clowes of the Heartland Foundation's *School Reform News* back in 2000.

That interview still stands up pretty well. Here are some of the things I said to Clowes:

> …we should make public education a little bit more like higher education. I think you accomplish that through the issuance of vouchers to every single student, bringing competition to public education and allowing children to choose schools much as they choose in higher education today.
> One of the huge criticisms of vouchers is that they're going to take money away from public education. Under my proposal—and I'll use this as the extreme example—if every child in Santa Fe were to take their school voucher and opt out of Santa Fe public

schools, the Santa Fe public schools would be left with about 35 percent of their budget and no students. It's just not going to happen, but it illustrates the point that as money for vouchers flows from the public schools, we actually raise the amount of money available for each student remaining in the public schools. That's because the public schools get $6,000 a student and we're granting a $4,000 voucher to those who choose outside the public school system.

During my first term as governor, New Mexico raised education spending by nearly one-third—and test scores and drop-out rates barely improved. That proved money wasn't the solution. It was time to shake up the system. By making children mobile, vouchers require schools to improve. Or lose students.

Before I began to speak out in favor of vouchers, about 35 percent of New Mexico's parents supported the idea; by early 2000, over 50 percent had come around to it.

One last observation: Some critics of school vouchers argue that they're racially- and culturally-biased because some groups of people lack a tradition of valuing education.

I think this argument is false.

When I was governor, the Native Americans in New Mexico were struggling with serious challenges in terms of public health, economic uncertainty and poor educational results. If any group could make legitimate claims about cultural bias in programs like school vouchers, it would be the tribes.

But the feedback I got from Native Americans on providing school alternatives was overwhelmingly positive. They were open to vouchers and anything else that would shake up the education *status quo* because they saw their schools as failed. Period.

To people in that position, choice is really important.

Seven Principles of Good Government

Execution is about preparation . . . and having enough experience to act calmly when action is required.

Chapter 10: Execution

Principle: Determine your goal, develop a plan and then execute it.

In 1989, I decided to run in the Leadville 100, a 100-mile marathon in Leadville, Colorado, where the elevation ranges from 10,000 to 13,000 feet. I didn't train, I just signed up knowing that the cut-off for the 100 miles was 30 hours. I wasn't trying to win, I just wanted to finish.

Things were going well until about mile 43 when my quads felt absolutely shot, really shot. Uphill was fine, it was downhill that was killing me. By mile 50, I thought I might have to drop out. But I just couldn't give up.

At mile 57, I started down a 13-mile decline, and my quads were so tight I didn't think there was any way I could go for another 33 miles uphill or downhill. Then I remembered a friend telling me about his experience on a 100-mile run. He ended up finishing by running backwards to give some relief to his quads.

So I tried it. I started running—walking might be more accurate—backwards down the hill. I was fine! I actually might win, I joked to myself. But I seriously started thinking that I might finish in 24 hours instead of 30.

Going backwards worked relatively wondrously until I hit mile 84. I couldn't go forwards or backwards anymore. But I couldn't quit because I had only 16 miles left to go. At the last aid station, with 11 miles left, I was crying in pain and thinking about the damage I was inflicting on my body.

The volunteers at the station asked how I was doing, and I put on a brave face so they wouldn't try to make me stop. When I got past them, I really cried. But I kept moving. It took me six hours and 45 minutes to go the last 16 miles, but I finished. With 15 minutes to spare.

There weren't too many people behind me, but I finished.

Emphasizing Growth

When I was governor, economic growth was one of my major goals, and I knew it could occur only if New Mexico's rural communities were connected with four-lane highways.

We needed a major improvement in infrastructure to thrive. By building 500 miles of four-lane highways, we could connect every town in the state with a population of at least 30,000. But the cost was prohibitive.

After exploring many options, we came up with a plan to maximize our return on investment by embracing private alternatives in building these roads. The highway project on Highway 44, which connects Albuquerque and Farmington, was designed, financed, built and guaranteed by a private company—which was revolutionary at the time.

This was completely unique. We were actually the first state in the nation to adopt an innovative financing program for Highway 44, by bonding future federal highway funds. Since then, other states have copied it and Wall Street embraced it.

The highway greatly boosted New Mexico's rural economies at the most competitive price.

Seven Principles of Good Government

Another goal was to reduce taxes. All taxes need to be as low as possible because politicians will spend whatever money they can get their hands on.

It became a habit of the New Mexico legislature to under-appropriate Medicaid by $100 million to $150 million every year so they could spend that money somewhere else. Then, when Medicaid needed more money—as it always did—they knew they could get it for such a politically correct cause.

I caught on to this game, and when they did it again, I vetoed $150 million of other appropriations to make up for the shortfall we knew would come.

When I started running marathons, training was hard. I forced myself to understand that, at first, running to the end of the block was a success. But I set my goal to be fit, and I've run more than 30 marathons.

I have an absolutely maniacal adherence to my goals and my belief when things happen, you can sit on the couch and watch or get up and deal with them head first.

During the Cerro Grande fire in May 2001, I spent many hours on the scene. As the *Denver Post* noted:

Gary Johnson was all over the Cerro Grande Fire. He helped reporters understand where the fire was headed when low-level Forest Service officials couldn't, ran herd over the bureaucratic process of getting state and federal agencies and the National Guard involved, and even helped put out some of the fire with his feet.

On a tour of Los Alamos, when he saw small flames spreading across a lawn, he…jumped out and stomped on the flames.

"You want to do something about this kind of thing. Then we realized there was a wall of fire in back of the house," he said. "The next thing you knew, you couldn't see your hand in front of your face. …In 12 minutes, the fire jumped both lines. I knew I was going to stay until Los Alamos was secure."

Executing on the Highest Level

My solution is to focus spending cuts on "the Big Four" government programs: Medicare, Medicaid, Social Security and Defense.

Seven Principles of Good Government

I favor federal government block grants to states to cover Medicaid and Medicare. Leave it up to the states to create programs that meet their residents' needs with a limited amount of money.

For Social Security, I believe that much could be accomplished toward assuring its long-term viability by raising the retirement age and a slight decrease in benefits, which I think might be accomplished by decreasing or deleting automatic annual benefit increases.

On Defense: We shouldn't have gone into Iraq and Afghanistan. But should we have 100,000 troops on the ground in Europe? Because America has been willing to be the world's policeman, other nations can afford infrastructure projects that the U.S. cannot. That doesn't make sense.

The alternative is for the United States economy to slide to third-world status. And the danger of a fundamental collapse is real.

On this point, here are some excerpts of a Q&A I did in August 2010 with the *Wall Street Journal's* "Washington Wire" blog:

> Forty-three cents on every dollar we're spending is borrowed and people are outraged over spending that's out of

control and the fact that taxes are going up across the board. It's my belief that we need to cut government spending by 43 percent.

…We're building roads, schools, bridges, highways and hospitals in Iraq and Afghanistan, and we're borrowing 43 cents in every dollar to do this.

And we have troops in Europe, we have troops in Japan, we have troops in South Korea.

Social Security, that really needs to be reformed. Medicaid probably needs to be capped when it comes to the states. Medicare, there needs to be some sort of means testing.

The [Social Security] retirement age needs to be raised. A portion of Social Security ought to be privatized, if not all. And there probably needs to be some means testing. It's a Ponzi scheme that's not sustainable.

It is fundamentally impossible to reduce the cost of government without reducing what government does. "Rolling back" spending to 2008 levels, imposing salary and hiring freezes, cutting "discretionary spending" by 5, 10 or even 20 percent—all those things are good efforts and prudent immediate steps.

However, if you do all those things without actually eliminating or reducing the countless things government does that we cannot afford, the result is that spending is simply deferred or juggled to get through the near-term crisis.

When Republicans took over Congress in the 1990s, they did so with the right ideas and right intentions. But, frankly, they blew it.

While they did some good things, when it came to fundamentally reducing what government does and how much it spends, they didn't solve the problem. They became *part* of it.

That can't happen this time around. The stakes are too high. Today, unlike in the 1990s, we are looking at deficits and debt that truly threaten to consume the U.S. economy, and which represent the single greatest threat to our national security.

Gary Johnson on Liberty, People and Politics

Biking through traffic. This is a perfect metaphor for governing. You need a clear idea of where you want to go . . . and you have to stay alert to a thousand things going on all around.

Seven Principles of Good Government

Behind the scenes at a campaign photo shoot. I've learned a lot about the importance of clear communication and a strong image in politics. And I'm learning more all the time.

Chapter 11: Communication

Principle: Communicate effectively.

The key ingredient—politically, professionally and personally—is communication. People stay connected through communication. In the early days of my business, we adopted what was a cutting-edge practice at the time by connecting all the key people via Motorola radio phones. Efficiency took a quantum leap. Business thrived. Employees were on the same page.

I learned early as a handyman that you had to know what customers expected and write it down. Communication was key. If I was going to be late—even five minutes late—I would call and let them know.

My most innovative mode of communication was my "Open Door After Four" program while I was governor. For eight straight years on the third Thursday of every month, I met with anyone from the state of New Mexico in five-minute increments from 4:00 p.m. until 10:00 p.m.

Some of these meetings were quite bizarre; others were unbelievably rich.

I got the idea from Governor Frank Keating of Oklahoma, and I know that Governor Bill Richardson continued it in New Mexico as well.

I can tell you that when I ran for reelection, no one knew more about the state than I did. It was like whistle-blowing without the attorney.

I knew about everything, everywhere. I was often able to change someone's life immensely and immediately and, in turn, fix the same problems for a lot of other people, too. No one could ever say that I wouldn't meet with him. Everyone could be heard.

One evening a trucker, who had driven millions of miles with no accidents, came in and showed me a picture of a truck going

under a railroad crossing bridge. He told me
the state had closed this underpass to truckers,
resulting in a several-hour detour every time
they took this route. He said the state was
claiming that the bridge was not high enough
to accommodate large trucks, but his years of
using the bridge and his picture showed this to
be untrue.

So I called the Transportation Department,
and the underpass was open to truckers the
next day with a sign that read, "Proceed at
Your Own Risk."

A couple of weeks later, I got a huge thank-
you card signed by 500 truckers.

When Communication Fails

As governor, I considered communication
paramount. And I learned its importance the
hard way.

A highly-publicized bill was coming through
the legislature, which would have allowed early
release of prisoners due to overcrowding. My
people actually went out and struck a deal with
the legislature but, partly because of a lack of
communication within my own staff, I didn't
agree to any of it.

When the bill passed, I vetoed it.

Some representatives (including a few who were potential allies for me) were outraged because it made them look soft on criminals.

This kind of miscommunication never happened again; my key people and I communicated much better after that.

We communicated much better with the legislators, too.

Non-Verbal Communication

Being on time also communicates an important message to me, a message of courtesy and respect.

As governor, I had a meeting scheduled one day at 10:00 a.m. with a group of Tribal Governors from various parts of the state. They didn't arrive until 10:45 a.m. When I sat down with them, I informed them that the meeting had been scheduled to be one hour long, so they had 15 minutes left. At 11:00 a.m., I adjourned the meeting.

They were never late again.

I am a stickler for punctuality. Being on time shows respect.

I've found that a lack of communication always results in mistakes or misunderstandings —in politics, in business and in relationships.

We need to say what's on our minds.

Working on Media Relations

Once I decided that I was going to run for White House in 2012, I made an effort to improve my communications with the mainstream media.

In January 2011, I wrote an article expressing some of my ideas about cutting the federal government's budget for the *Daily Caller*.

Here are a few of the things I had to say:

> News reports have been full of debates about whether it is feasible to cut $100 billion, for example, from federal spending this year—as some have advocated. Even among committed, well-intentioned conservatives, we heard far too much equivocating and qualifying of that prospect.
>
> $100 billion? We can get to that number without breaking a sweat—if we just decide to do it. The government spends $25 billion a year maintaining vacant federal property. If it's vacant, sell it, tear it down, or give it away, but stop spending the $25 billion.

We are spending $10 billion a year
on government travel. [The president
should] send a memo tomorrow
directing everyone to cut their trips in
half. I suspect few of us taxpayers would
notice the difference, and there is $5
billion in savings right there. Tomorrow.
Remember all that stimulus money
Congress appropriated? Guess what: $50
or $60 billion of it hasn't been spent yet.
…Congress should simply repeal that
unspent stimulus money. Now, before
it's gone.

There is another $10 to $20 billion
sitting around in government accounts
that was appropriated two or three years
ago, but has not yet been obligated.
With a simple vote and a stroke of the
president's pen, those dollars could be
rescinded. Today.

There was so much agitation and debate
in Washington over $100 billion in spending
cuts in a year. We just did it on this page—and
could see real benefits in weeks. Not years.

Here's what *The Atlantic* magazine
noted around the time of my speech to the

Gary Johnson on Liberty, People and Politics

Conservative Political Action Conference (CPAC) in early 2011:

> Having served two terms as governor of New Mexico—one more term in office than Mitt Romney, and one-and-a-half more than Sarah Palin—his biggest boast is that he vetoed 750 bills and over a billion dollars of spending from 1994 to 2002. He talks the fiscal-conservative talk as well as anyone out there. ...
>
> "My entire life, I've just always thought that this is just not sustainable, and that at some point the bill would be due," he told me when I interviewed him before a speaking appearance at American University late last month. "I just think that that day is right now, finally."
>
> This is the stuff every Republican primary voter seems to want to hear: Earnest appreciation of deficit catastrophe, and pledges to address the problem with drastic reductions in government spending. ...A marijuana legalizer will probably not win the White House any time soon. Johnson himself says the nation is two years away from a tipping point on the issue, when it stops

> being "the one issue you can't talk about
> and get elected."
>
> According to that timeline, the tipping
> point will occur several months after the
> 2012 Election Day.

I really want to take a hard look at the
war on drugs in this country and to include
legalization as a potential alternative.

One of the longest profiles that the
mainstream media has done on me appeared
in the November 2011 issue of *GQ* magazine.
Here are a few high points of that one:

> The man is frugal beyond belief. "But
> I am not cheap." ...He likes to think
> he spends his own money the way he'd
> spend the country's money: Pay only for
> quality and don't waste a cent. Like, for
> instance, stop pissing away money on
> border patrols and erecting fences and
> walls across the Mexican border, and let
> immigrants earn work visas "and actually
> contribute to our economy." And while
> he's on the topic of wasteful spending,
> he says there'll be no pleasure trips to
> the Vineyard on Air Force One.

When I started giving lots of interviews
with national media, in early 2010, that was

really a soft opening. I'm a lot sharper now—
and, as my campaign goes on, I'm going to be
sharper still.

It's the same process I used when I
successfully ran for governor. And I know I
won't be viable unless I can provide a level of
specificity in my communication. And this is
true for anyone seeking the presidency.

I'm not going to change what I believe, but
I am going to communicate it better.

Seven Principles of Good Government

Early in my tenure as governor, when I was still getting used to having my picture taken all the time. And dealing with a 24/7 job. I soon learned how important it is to have bad news delivered immediately; if you do, you can react in a timely manner.

Chapter 12: Courage

Principle: Anything that will be revealed eventually should be revealed immediately.

Don't hesitate to deliver bad news.

I didn't need to reveal my past drug use. I guess I could have waited until someone found out or asked, hoping they never would. But I was so turned off by President Bill Clinton's statement that he'd smoked marijuana but didn't inhale.

Come on!

I wanted to be honest about it, so I volunteered the information. I have also been open about what made me quit.

I am proud to say that there was no scandal of any kind in my administration as governor.

One of the keys to success is surrounding yourself with the right people. I chose great people. That isn't to say that they didn't make mistakes or that I didn't have to get rid of those who weren't working.

I found that firing people was the hardest thing I had to do in business. I also learned that letting the wrong people stay was hard, too. Sometimes I would give people two, three, or even four chances to make the grade—but I found they rarely changed.

In most cases, if people don't work the first time, they never will.

Courage as Accountability

Based on my experience in business, I vowed as governor that I wouldn't let people slide. I would give them a limited time to work out, and if they didn't, they had to leave. I wouldn't let it linger.

I found that those whom I fired felt they had a new lease on life. They were not performing or enjoying their work, so letting them go was actually a blessing in disguise for both sides.

Gary Johnson on Liberty, People and Politics

As governor, I held weekly meetings with my Cabinet. I told them every week that if they didn't work out, I didn't have time to waste. I would replace them.

I also told them that if they were still here, I had confidence in them and the jobs they were doing.

The result: They all felt they were high performers, proud of the jobs they were doing.

In our weekly meetings, each Cabinet member was required to give a three-minute presentation on their department. I could easily tell in those three minutes who was doing a great job and who was coasting along.

There were no surprises. Every member of my Cabinet and I could tell you who the weakest member was.

I told my Cabinet members from the beginning that they could disagree with me, but they had to at least understand my positions.

This created a problem with my Secretary of Public Safety, Darren White, whom I'd taken to Washington, D.C. to meet with a group of international drug-reform leaders. I wanted him to understand my position on the legalization of marijuana, and I figured he would learn a lot by hearing from the experts.

Later, he got a vote of no confidence from the State Police and, the very afternoon that a major drug conference was to take place in Albuquerque, he resigned. *Disappointment* hardly described my feelings.

But the worst part of it was reading in the paper that White said he "had no idea where the governor was coming from."

He did! I'd made sure of it.

The Courage to Fix Problems

The only Cabinet member I had to fire was my Economic Development Secretary. I hired him on a Wednesday, and on Thursday he took the state plane to his home in Las Cruces for the weekend. Without telling me.

He'd also lied on his resume, saying he had earned some sort of degree.

Which he hadn't.

I feel I've mostly done a good job hiring people. In business and in public service. But, if I make a personnel mistake, I fix it quickly.

For me, as governor of New Mexico, everything was a cost-benefit analysis. There weren't any sacred cows—everything was a cost-benefit analysis. What are we spending money on and what are we getting for the money that we're spending? So, in that sense, the drug war is absolutely a failure.

I think we should balance the federal budget tomorrow. I'm optimistic. I think Americans are optimistic. We went to the moon, we can balance the federal budget. We can fix this. But we're not addressing the problems that we face—and that starts with Medicaid, Medicare, Social Security and Defense.

And I mean we actually need to *cut* budgets in those areas.

How Courage Affects Your Life

Courage isn't boastful. In fact, it's more often humble. And humbling.

Nothing confirms that fact to me more than the trouble I had on my way back down from the summit of Mt. Everest.

As I explained in a short interview with the Associated Press, published in June 2003, just after I got back:

> Johnson says he thought he was going to die when part of an icefall collapsed during his descent from the summit of Mount Everest.
>
> "That was the scariest part of the whole thing," he said.

Johnson, who made it to the 29,035-foot summit May 30, said he and fellow climber Dave Hahn were on top of the Khumbu Icefall when it collapsed. "We can't see it. We can just hear it, and it's close. We hear the crash. ...We were certain we were dead, that it was going to domino. It was petrifying."
The icefall, which is constantly shifting, is a glacier pitched over a precipitous drop at 20,000 feet on Everest.

Courage influences public policy in all kinds of ways—directly and indirectly.

For example: Immigration is an issue on which most of the so-called "mainstream" politicians in the United States have shown a striking *lack* of courage.

In a 2010 interview with the Irish journalist Niall Stanage (published in the U.S. by the news and opinion web site Salon.com), I was able to share some of my ideas on immigration policy:

Johnson doesn't bother to hide his disdain for [Republican] hard-liners. Take the incendiary new immigration law passed in Arizona, for instance: "I just don't think it's going to work," he says. "I think it's going to lead to

racial profiling. I don't know how
you determine one individual from
another—is it color of skin?—as to
whether one is an American citizen or
the other is an illegal immigrant."

Stanage noted, rightly, that I favor
an expansive guest worker program and
am uncomfortable with the idea of mass
deportation.

So, he asked me about the idea of
increasing security by means of a border wall.

"I have never been supportive of the wall,"
I answered. "A 10-foot wall just requires an 11-
foot ladder."

With my parents at an Albuquerque Triathlon event. My father paid me one of the best compliments I've ever received: He said I actually do the things I talk about.

Chapter 13: Integrity

Principle: Find a job you love and make a difference.

Reality dictates that we must work. Because of the amount of time we spend working, I believe that finding a job you love should be at the top of everyone's priority list. Doing something you love should be a rule of life.

It was fun to make as much money as I did running Big J Enterprises. I loved fulfilling my goal of making enough money to achieve freedom, but I didn't always love the job.

In one year, I made five times as much money as my parents both made in their entire lifetimes. I learned that money is not happiness, however. It wasn't all that magical.

What do you do with money? How many cars can you buy? You can only live in one house at a time.

Isn't what we're after to love what we do?

I love what I do. I love being free. I loved being governor. I loved making money as a small business owner. I love a 24/7, blood-boiling challenge—which is what running for president is for me. The challenge, the adrenaline rush, the chance to make the world a better place is riveting.

I've adopted the approach of living in the moment because I believe that's what we're really after. I get it skiing, mountaineering, biking. Getting a job you love is living in the present, being in the moment. That's the magic in life. Don't we owe that to ourselves?

When I first enjoyed a level of financial success that I had never dreamed of, it was very confusing. Because the reality was—guess what?—bells and whistles don't go off all day long. They don't.

No matter how much money you have in the bank, you still have to get up every morning. You still have to put your shoes on.

You still have to eat.

I can say with certainty that financial success isn't the key to life.

The key to life, what it's all about, is *enjoying* the things you do everyday.

Some people ask me about my "zen" approach to governing. I think these questions come from an interview I did that appeared in *The Atlantic* in April 2011. Here's what I said:

> I really think that life is about being in a state of zen. If I might describe zen for you, it's being in the moment. The thing that gets someone there might be music, art, golf, reading, writing. It might be a job that you have.
>
> For me, I've found it in athletics. And I've also found it in politics.
>
> ...In my twenties I would put so much emphasis on winning an athletic event itself. But I came to a reckoning many years ago. Life became a process. I thought, I really enjoy being fit. I really enjoy the moments it takes to stay fit. I try to always enjoy the moment—I am enjoying this conversation. I don't want to be anyplace else. You'd like to win. But more important is that you've

established yourself as someone who is capable of winning. It's not that I went to Mount Everest and summitted. That was terrific. But I got to go to Everest in the first place. I was fit enough. I had enough resources. I had enough moxie, if you will, to be there and attempt this thing. So that's life. For me, athletics is in the moment. For me, governing is in the moment too.

Being governor was a blood-boiling job. It was 24/7. On hundreds of issues, I got to be in the middle of understanding them.

What I liked was the process. The learning, the deliberation, the decision-making—putting it all together, and asking, "Given these options, what is in the public's interest? How can we get that done?"

It was an "in the moment" experience.

When I was governor, this is what I told everybody in my cabinet:

You can disagree with me every day of the week, and you can do it in front of the media, as long as you say, "Here is the governor's position, and here is my position. And here is why I disagree with the governor."

If I was out running, I didn't want my staff telling anybody that I was in some sort of meeting. Tell them that I'm out running!

Integrity and the Law

In an article that ran in a December 2010 issue of the *Weekly Standard*, I spoke with reporter John McCormack about a few issues, including smoking marijuana after my paragliding accident:

> It's not anything I volunteer, but you're the only person that actually asked about it. But for luck, I guess, I wasn't arrested.

Smoking marijuana for medicinal purposes was illegal in New Mexico until 2007.

> I'd suffered multiple bone fractures, including a burst fracture to my T12 vertebrae. In my human experience, it's the worst pain I've ever felt. Rather than using painkillers, which I have used on occasion before, I did smoke pot.

I realize that staying true to my beliefs sometimes puts me against conventional notions of justice. And law. But I'm used to that tension.

As I've said in several interviews: Damn the polls. I move them.

Seven Principles of Good Government

Nobody has asked me to run for president, and I cannot think of a bigger challenge. I always hear politicians say they're being called to duty or sacrificing for their country.

Not me.

What could be a more interesting challenge than to change the world in a positive way? Life is about experiences, and I revel in the experience of running for president.

I think my Principles of Good Government will make the world a better place, and I wouldn't seek the presidency if I didn't think I could do a good job.

One of hundreds of Q&A sessions. Citizens all around the U.S. have a sense that something's not right about how the federal government is operating. It's doing too much.

Gary Johnson on Liberty, People and Politics

A great meeting of students at the University of Iowa. They played music, listened to a number of speakers (including me) and made the case for individual liberty.

Seven Principles of Good Government

Restoring liberty in America is serious business.

Conclusion

In my campaign for president, I am running as a non-politician. Again. My political disengagement since serving as governor of New Mexico makes my message clearer, not muddied or muffled or part of the background noise. But it's blood-boiling to be engaged in what I view to be the ultimate challenge of running for president. It's high octane and fun.

For me, it's not going to be about winning. The victory is to be engaged. For me, it's a win just to be involved.

A few days after Christmas 2011, I appeared at a press conference in Santa Fe to announce that I would seek the Libertarian Party's nomination for president in 2012. Here's how the *Manchester Union-Leader* reported on the conference:

> Former New Mexico Gov. Gary Johnson has left the Republican Party, stating he will instead seek the Libertarian Party presidential nomination. ...The Libertarian Party nominee will appear on the presidential ballot in all 50 states. In announcing the switch, Johnson stated he was disappointed with the treatment he received in the GOP. Johnson was invited to take part in just two GOP presidential debates. "It was both a difficult decision, and an easy one," said Johnson. "It was difficult because I have a lot of Republican history, and a lot of Republican supporters. But in the final analysis, as many, many commentators have said since watching how I governed New Mexico, I am a Libertarian."

And this is what the *Daily Caller* (which has given me some good coverage in the past) had to say:

> Americans who favor the legalization of marijuana and same-sex marriage, and also want a balanced federal budget and

restrained foreign policy, now have an alternative to the two major parties in 2012.

During a press conference at the state capitol in Santa Fe, former New Mexico Gov. Gary Johnson announced that he was dropping his bid for the GOP nomination and running for president instead as a Libertarian Party candidate. "The Libertarian Party nominee will be on the ballot in all 50 states," Johnson said. "That is very significant."

The *Caller* noted that—right out of the blocks—I was running strong in a three-way race in New Mexico:

A recent Public Policy Polling survey showed Johnson, running as a Libertarian, with 23 percent support in the state in a hypothetical match up against former Massachusetts Governor Mitt Romney and President Obama. ... Regarding the possibility of a third-party run watering down Republican electoral strength, Johnson told TheDC that he would expect to deprive President Obama of just as many votes as he would the GOP nominee.

And I still believe that.

I've always felt life's highest calling was doing good by other people; and I've always felt that politics was a way of elevating that calling. This was what I hoped my life would be about, to be in a position to make a difference.

I have had enough of big-government politicians and where they are taking our country. I want to step up, be heard and get this country back on track as a vehicle for individuals to achieve their dreams.

Let's reconnect with freedom and liberty.

I opposed the Iraq War from the start. I support Federal Reserve transparency. I believe in a woman's right to choose. I support the legalization of marijuana. And I was the only sitting Republican governor not to endorse George W. Bush in his first presidential run.

Here's what the *National Review* had to say, in a January 2011 interview that appeared on its web site:

> If Gary Johnson were president, he would immediately cut all federal spending—entitlements, defense, education, everything—by 43 percent to rectify our fiscal blunders. And he'd just be getting started.

What is [Johnson's] philosophy? In two words: limited government.

…He suggests that to encourage fiscal discipline, the federal government should pass a law that lays out a process for state bankruptcies—which are impossible under current law and would be hard to square with sovereign immunity—and makes it clear that federal bailouts are off the table. "Everybody would scream" if a state went into bankruptcy, Johnson admits, but a federal bailout would only encourage profligacy.

I'm a fix-it man. Within two terms as governor, I'd eliminated New Mexico's budget deficit and cut the rate of state government growth in half while reducing the state workforce by over 10 percent, without laying off a single qualified state worker.

America needs a "President Veto" right now—someone who will say "no" to insane spending and stop the madness that has become Washington.

Seven Principles of Good Government

Appendix

In the last few years, leading up to my 2012 campaign, I started and ran a think tank called the Our America Initiative (its web site is www.ouramericainitiative.com). It allowed me to refine some key policy positions. In this Appendix, you can read some of these.

Abortion

I support a woman's right to choose.

Civil Liberties

The government should protect the value of individuals and their civil liberties. It should not intervene in the private lives of individual citizens unnecessarily. Personal liberty and freedom from unwarranted governmental control or regulation should allow law abiding individuals to pursue their own desires as long as they are not causing harm to other people. There should be "less government, greater liberty and lasting prosperity for America."

While many of our liberties are threatened by a government grown too large and too intrusive, there are some fundamental freedoms that are under particular threat. The Patriot Act, for example, is a direct assault on both privacy and the due processes of law. It should be repealed.

Marriage equality is another right that I believe to be protected by the Constitution's basic guarantees. It is simply not right that the government tells Americans who they can or cannot marry under the law. Religions and individuals with strongly-held beliefs should be free to define marriage as they wish; however, those definitions have no place in creating discrimination when it comes to allowing the legal benefits of marriage to some, while denying them to others.

Constitution

I believe that the Constitution should be interpreted according to its original meaning.

After great deliberation, the Founders clearly based the blueprint for our government on the fundamental idea that there must be strict constraints on federal power—an idea from which we have strayed much too far.

I believe that the proper balance needs to be restored between the different branches of government. This includes the rights of states.

Defense and the Middle East War

The federal government's most basic responsibility is that of protecting us from those who would do us harm. To the men and women of the military who fulfill that responsibility each and every day, we owe our support and gratitude.

To provide for the security of its citizens, the United States should pursue a foreign policy of non-intervention—but not isolationism. We must not engage in military conflicts or the affairs of sovereign nations when there is no clear U.S. interest or threat.

The war in Iraq was a costly mistake which has resulted in the unintended consequences of an empowered Iran and damaged relationships across the Middle East. In Afghanistan, we accomplished the initial and justified mission of uprooting al Qaeda and those who attacked us on 9/11 in a matter of months, and should have brought our troops home years ago, rather than engaging in the doomed-to-fail and unjustified nation-building that continues today.

Our troops in Afghanistan should be withdrawn immediately.

By shifting our military's mission from one of intervention and "offense" to its constitutional and proper mission of defense, we can and must dramatically reduce military spending—without compromising national security.

With the federal government borrowing (or printing) 43 cents of every dollar it spends, foreign aid is a luxury we simply cannot afford. There are roads, bridges and schools to be built here in the United States, but which we cannot afford. We certainly cannot afford to do so in other countries.

We must not, however, confuse non-intervention and an end to nation-building with isolationism. The use of key strategic alliances, such as our relationship with Israel, can enhance our economic and national-security interests, while saving American tax dollars.

Drug Policy

Drug abuse is harmful to individual lives and society as a whole. The war on drugs as waged over the past few decades, however, is a massive failure. Crime, costs to society and substance abuse itself have not been reduced, yet we continue to overwhelm the courts, law enforcement and government at all levels by treating drug use as a criminal issue rather than the health issue it is.

New approaches are needed. An important first step is the legalization and regulation of marijuana. Doing so will not only strike a major blow to the profits and criminal incentives of the cartels but will also end the insanity of arresting, prosecuting and punishing millions of Americans each year for using marijuana.

Prohibition didn't work the first time, and it is certainly not working today.

For other drugs, I advocate a shift to harm reduction strategies that will address abuse as a health problem—not a never-ending criminal justice burden.

Economy

Free markets and limited government are the foundation of prosperity. Economic policy should foster entrepreneurship, innovation, and individual choice, not direct economic activity to satisfy political interests in Washington.

Americans should be free to make their own economic decisions because individuals, not government, know what is best for themselves and their families. This freedom unleashes the creativity and enterprising spirit that fuels economic opportunity and an equal playing field for all Americans.

To allow prosperity, the U.S. must:

- Slash spending. Borrowing 43 cents of every dollar government spends is simply unsustainable. Spending must be reduced immediately to eliminate deficit spending and begin the task of paying down our debt, without increasing the tax burden on individuals and businesses.

- Eliminate taxes that penalize earning, investment and savings. The current tax system does all the wrong things. It discourages investment, penalizes productivity, and places the U.S. at a competitive disadvantage in the world marketplace. We should abolish the IRS and adopt a simple, consumption-based tax system to replace individual income taxes, capital gains taxes, payroll taxes and corporate taxes.

- Stop government from picking winners and losers in the marketplace. Through a ridiculous maze of tax credits and subsidies, as well as regulatory schemes designed not to provide basic protections, but to "manage" business and personal behavior, the government is directly involved in virtually every aspect of the private economy. That leads only to inefficiency, unfairness, corruption and diminished prosperity. By eliminating the current tax system and allowing a truly level playing field for entrepreneurs, investors, workers and the marketplace at large, millions of jobs will be created and economic decision-making will be returned to its proper place: Buyers, sellers and producers acting in an environment free from manipulation by the government.

Environment

A clean and safe environment is critical to us and to future generations. Government's role in protecting that environment is a fundamental one of protecting us from those who would do us harm. That, however, does not require the government to "manage" the environment by attempting to reward or penalize us in order to direct our behaviors in the marketplace, in our homes, or in our lives. "Cap-and-trade" and other tax schemes, regardless of what they are called, will do little or nothing to improve the environment—while imposing costs we cannot afford.

Effective, long-term environmental stewardship and conservation are impossible without a healthy economy and the freedom to make responsible decisions.

Federal Reserve

Misguided efforts by the Federal Reserve in recent years to manipulate the economy have accomplished the opposite of its original, fundamental responsibilities: protecting the value of our currency and assuring price stability. Rather, the value of our money has been reduced and wealth destroyed.

The activities and priorities of the Fed must be reviewed, its conduct made transparent not only to Congress, but to the American people.

Do away with the Federal Reserve's dual role: managing the currency *and* trying to manage full employment.

Health Care

Government has never managed any segment of the economy successfully. To expect that it can do so for health care—one of the largest segments—is insanity. Nowhere is it more important that the best possible services and products be available at affordable prices than in the area of health. Government simply cannot fulfill that mission. Rather, real competition, freedom to innovate and a working marketplace will provide Americans with the health care they want and will demand.

To the extent that we, as a society, want to help those who are truly in need, that help can best be provided by the states—with any federal assistance coming in the form of block grants to be applied to best practices, innovative programs and the most efficient delivery of services.

Immigration

Real border security means knowing who is entering the country and why. It does not mean fences, profiling or the militarization of the boundaries we share with other nations.

A market-based system for issuing work visas for those who want to come here and work will allow a safe, manageable and economically beneficial flow of people into and out of the country—and dramatically reduce the number of "illegal" entries by those who simply cannot navigate the current unworkable system.

For those who are already here illegally, having either entered illegally or overstayed visas, a common-sense grace period during which they can leave the shadows of society and apply for temporary legal status is both a humane and logical approach.

Legal immigration is a key element of our economic well-being. It should be encouraged and facilitated, not rendered unrealistic by an outdated and bureaucratic system that does not meet the needs of the marketplace or those who want to come here to pursue their dreams.